Hello God
It's Me

Stephanie King • Helen Mahood

Scripture Union

© Text: Stephanie King
© Illustrations: Helen Mahood
First Published 2001

Scripture Union, 207–209 Queensway, Bletchley, Milton Keynes MK2 2EB, England

ISBN 1 85999 462 8

All rights reserved. No part of this publication may be reproduced, stored in a retrieval system, or transmitted in any form or by any means, electronic, mechanical, photocopying, recording or otherwise, without the prior permission of Scripture Union.

The right of Stephanie King to be identified as author of this work has been asserted by her in accordance with the Copyright, Designs and Patents Act 1988.

Scriptures quoted from The Good News Bible published by The Bible Societies/Harper Collins Publishers Ltd., UK © American Bible Society 1966, 1971, 1976, 1992, used with permission.

British Library Cataloguing-in-Publication Data.
A catalogue record of this book is available from the British Library.

Printed and bound in Singapore by Tien Wah Press.

Contents

Prayers about my family	5
Prayers about learning	12
Prayers about travelling	18
Prayers about playing	24
Prayers about eating	30
Prayers about growing	32
Morning and evening prayers	38
Prayers about special times	44

*For my dad, whose big hands always
pulled me up life's hillsides*

PRAYERS ABOUT MY FAMILY

Photographs

We have a book full of photos —
pictures of us
— my sister and me in the bath,
— Mum and Dad getting married,
— Gran and Grandpa in hats,
(that photo is dusty and brown)
our whole history in a book.

God knows it all, and was there too.
He knows all about yesterday,
he knows all about tomorrow, and
the photos we will take tomorrow.

Thank you, God,
that you will be there tomorrow with me.
Amen.

Prayers about my family

My dad

My dad's hand is much bigger than mine,
it's warm and strong.
When I'm climbing a hill
but can't go any further,
Dad grabs my hand
and we run up together.
I laugh all the way.

Thank you, Heavenly Father,
that your hands are strong and loving.
You hold my hand and pull me along
when life seems like a steep hill.
Amen.

Prayers about my family

Granny and Grandpa

"How many times have I wanted to put my arms round all your people, just as a hen gathers her chicks under her wings."
               Matthew chapter 23, verse 37

Granny and Grandpa live a long way away,
but when we go to stay with them
they are close and I can give them a hug.
Please be with my granny and grandpa, Lord Jesus.
Stay with them,
give them a hug,
look after them for me.
Amen.

Prayers about my family

Me

Look in the mirror —
Who's that?
ME!!
Nobody else in the whole wide world
has a face exactly like mine.
My eyes
my hair
my nose
my teeth
my smile.

My face is special because I'm special.
God made me just right
because he loves me.
ME!!
Thank you, God,
Amen.

Prayers about my family

Kisses

If kisses came in boxes
I would have used all mine up by now.
Grown-ups always make you kiss
whether you want to or not.

Kiss hallo,
kiss goodbye,
kiss for Auntie,
kiss for Granny,
kiss night-night.

Really, God,
it's a good job you made it easy to give kisses.
I seem to need so many
every day.
Amen.

Prayers about my family

My mum

Mum! Mummy!!

The room is dark,
and my duvet slipped off.
I had a nightmare.
I'm cold and frightened and alone.

But when I shout
my mum is quick to come.
There are arms to comfort,
gentle words,
love that makes me feel safe.

Thank you, Heavenly Father,
for the people who love me
and hold me when I'm sad.
Amen.

Prayers about my family

New baby

Mum's come home from the hospital with a new baby!!
Tiny and crinkly,
black hair and fat cheeks,
a big mouth that cries and sucks and yells.
When I give him my finger, he holds on tight.
Does he know it's me?
His eyes open and I say hello.

I think I like having a new baby.
Thank you, God, for making him so new and tiny and perfect.
Amen.

PRAYERS ABOUT LEARNING

Counting hairs

Jesus said: "As for you, even the hairs of your head have all been counted. So do not be afraid..."
Matthew chapter 10 verses 30–31

I can't begin to count all my hairs!!
There are tens, hundreds, thousands, millions!!
It's impossible!!

Yet you, Father, made me, every bit.
You made all my hairs, one by one,
and counted them.

Thank you, Father, for knowing all about me
and caring about every tiny part of my life.
Help me to tell you about the things that worry me,
even the things that are too small to tell anyone else.
Make me always sure of your love for me.
Amen.

Prayers about learning

In the playground

Sometimes it can be scary in the playground.
So many children rushing around,
big boys with heavy backpacks,
big girls running and not looking,
everyone in groups with their friends.

I'm on my own.
I don't know anyone.

Lord Jesus, be with me in the playground.
Please help me to be brave.
Please help me to find a friend.
Amen.

Prayers about learning

Painting

At school we do painting.
There are big pots of paint,
yellow, red, orange and blue,
big fat brushes,
big pieces of white paper.

I put on an apron,
take a brush.
Squiggles, swirls, dots and lines.
"Look!" I show my teacher,
but the paint slides off the paper,
all down my apron!

I love painting,
and making pictures to take home.
Thank you very much, Lord Jesus,
for the lovely paint.
Amen.

Prayers about learning

Bible stories

"Jesus used parables to tell them many things."
Matthew chapter 13, verse 3

On Sundays we read a Bible story
— often it's a story that Jesus told.
Did you like telling stories, Jesus?
People must have loved hearing them,
because everyone loves a story.
I'd like to sit next to you,
and you would tell a story just for me.

Thank you for understanding us, Lord Jesus,
for telling us stories that teach us about you.
Amen.

Prayers about learning

Using words

I've heard lots of words today –
friendly words,
funny words,
shouted words,
bad words,
angry words,
busy words.

But in the Bible
your words to the people you love are
story words,
thoughtful words,
understanding words,
smiling words,
kind words.

I am sure that you love me
and your words to me are kind.
Thank you for your love
and your kindness.
Amen.

Prayers about learning

Telling the time

At school there's a clock
and we're learning to tell the time.
It's very complicated —
seconds, minutes, hours, days,
weeks, months, years, centuries,
even a millennium.

I'm very glad, Father God,
that you are the one who started time,
that one day you'll stop time,
that you're in charge of time.
Amen.

PRAYERS ABOUT TRAVELLING

The sea

Jumping waves is brilliant!
Cold around my toes,
salty on my lips,
glittering in my eyes.
Thank you for making waves so
green and shiny and bubbly,
always another one coming,
always different.
Thank you for making the sea
so AMAZING!
Amen.

Prayers about travelling

On the bus

It always seems cold when we go to the bus.
It's cold walking to the bus stop,
cold waiting for the bus to come,
cold legs, cold fingers, cold nose.

But when the bus comes,
it's warm and steamy inside.
Everyone chats and it feels happy.
I like drawing stick men
on the foggy windows.
I can nearly write my name backwards.

So thank you for the good bits of buses
and help me not to moan
when it's cold!
Amen.

Prayers about travelling

Rainy fun

Suddenly it rained today.
Huge drops fell out of the sky.
So much rain,
so fast,
crashing on our heads, faces, shoulders.
I pulled my T-shirt over my head
but then my back got all wet!

Mum and I raced to the car.
Our feet got soaked in the puddles,
water dripped down my hair into my ears,
Mum's glasses had drops all over.

It was fun in the rain –
a sudden adventure.
Thank you, Lord,
Amen.

Prayers about travelling

Sparrows

Jesus said: "For only a penny you can buy two sparrows, yet not one sparrow falls to the ground without your Father's consent... So do not be afraid; you are worth much more than many sparrows!"
Matthew chapter 10, verses 29–31

One morning we found a sparrow
lying dead by the side of the road.
It was very tiny, and nobody cared except us;
nobody had even noticed.
I'm so glad, Father, that you know about every sparrow,
that you care about every single tiny bird!
You know all about ME too,
and I know you will take care of me.
Amen.

Prayers about travelling

Holidays

Thank you, Jesus,
for our wonderful holiday.
No school!
We got up in the dark
and had breakfast in the car.
Mum's happy, and Dad's singing.
We're going to sleep in a real tent,
go swimming in the sea!

Thank you, Lord Jesus,
for giving us this lovely holiday.
Amen.

Prayers about travelling

A starry night

"In the beginning... God created the universe."
Genesis chapter 1, verse 1

We came home late one night.
Outside it was cold and very dark
but Dad said, "Look!"
and up in the sky all the stars were crisp and bright,
patterns and pictures in crunchy diamonds
against the black sky.
We stood and looked.

Dad said, "God is bigger
than all the stars.
He made the planets,
the moon, and the earth,
and the sun
yet he knows all about us!"
Isn't that amazing?
Wow! Thank you, Lord.
Amen.

PRAYERS ABOUT PLAYING

Playing with friends

It's great in the playground,
swinging round the bars,
running across the grass,
racing little cars down the hill,
being planes in the wind.
Thank you, Father, for my friends
and all the fun we have together.
Amen.

Falling over

My knees are scratched,
my hands are bleeding,
I feel wobbly all over,
I hurt.
I didn't mean to fall over
and it happened so quickly.

Please make my sore hands better soon.
Please help me to be brave.
Amen.

Prayers about playing

Laughter

Laughing can make your tummy hurt!
Sometimes I can't stop laughing
when my friend tells me funny jokes,
when my sister tickles me,
when I watch cartoons on TV.
I like laughing.

Thank you, Lord Jesus, for all the things that make me laugh.
Thank you that we laugh a lot.
Amen.

My best friend

My friend says that she doesn't want
to be my best friend any more.
Why not? I still like her.

Lord Jesus, please help me to be her friend,
even when she's not friendly to me.
Amen.

Prayers about playing

Being sorry

"Why, then, do you look at the speck in your brother's eye, and pay no attention to the log in your own eye?"
Matthew chapter 7, verse 3

It was her fault!
She pushed me,
she got in the way,
she messed up the game.

Not me –
it wasn't my fault.
Well, perhaps just a bit...
Perhaps quite a lot....

I'm sorry, I think it was my fault too.
Please forgive me, Lord Jesus.
Please show me how to play better next time.
Amen.

Prayers about playing

New boots

Thank you for my boots, Lord Jesus,
new and shiny and red.
SPLISH in the puddles,
SPLASH in the gutters,
SPLOSH all over my mum!
Water everywhere
but my feet are dry!
Great!
Thank you, Lord Jesus, for my new red boots.
Amen.

Outdoor fun

I can spread my arms,
jump up high,
run fast,
shout out loud.

I can feel the sun!
I'm outdoors!
Thank you, God,
for this beautiful day!
Amen.

Prayers about playing

A special person

If I could have a friend, Jesus,
it would be really nice.
Please could I have someone to play with?
We could do things together
and I wouldn't be on my own.

We could practise football,
play games on the computer,
have races on our bikes.

A special person,
my own friend.
Thanks.
Amen.

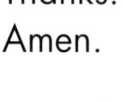

Prayers about playing

Flying a kite

"The wind blows wherever it wishes; you hear the sound it makes, but you do not know where it comes from or where it is going."
John chapter 3, verse 8

Today was very windy
and Dad said,
"Let's go fly your new kite."
At the top of the hill
the wind was strong and cold.
Up went my kite into the sky,
flapping away,
twisting and looping,
then crashing to the ground.

Where does the wind go?
Where does it come from?
I don't know,
but I'm sure that you do know, God.
Amen.

PRAYERS ABOUT EATING

Our tea

Thank you, Lord Jesus, for our tea today —
hamburgers, chips and peas.
You ate fish and bread.
I don't like fish
so thank you for my hamburger!
Amen.

Good food

Thank you, Lord,
for the smell of delicious dinner cooking,
for the sound of knives and forks on the table,
for the sight of good food,
for the taste of my favourite meal!
Amen.

Prayers about eating

Favourite food

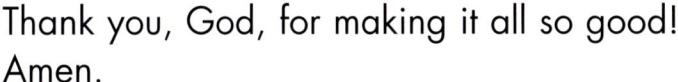

Cake, hot from the oven,
casserole, brown and dark,
strawberries and sugar, smelling of summer,
ice cream, freezing on my teeth,
apples, crunchy and cold.

Thank you, God, for making it all so good!
Amen.

All our food

Fast food,
favourite food,
feast food,
for all our food,
we thank you, Father.
Amen.

PRAYERS ABOUT GROWING

Growing up

I wonder what I'll be when I grow up?

Perhaps a nurse?
 (I like doing bandages)
Or an astronaut?
 (floating in space would be cool)
Somebody who tries out new chocolates in a factory?
 (mmm)
Or a plumber, bending copper pipes round corners?
A park ranger, looking after bears?

Whatever I'll be, I'll still be ME!
Thank you, God.
Amen.

Prayers about growing

Tight shoes

"Can any of you grow a bit taller by worrying about it?"
Luke chapter 12, verse 25

Suddenly my shoes feel tight,
my toes touch the end,
there's no space left to wiggle.

Did my shoes get smaller?
Perhaps they shrank in the rain?
Perhaps my feet got bigger?
It's funny that I can't feel them growing.
I can't make them grow.

It must be you, God, who makes my feet big.
You know that I'm little
and I need to be bigger,
so slowly, slowly, you're changing me.

Thank you, God.
Amen.

Prayers about growing

Wobbly teeth

Lord Jesus, do you know what happened today?
My wobbly tooth fell out!
The one at the front
that I could wiggle with my tongue!

Now I have a gap —
it feels soft and funny
with a hard sharp bit
that mum says is my new tooth.

I'm really growing up now!
I'm getting grown-up teeth!
Thank you!
Amen.

Prayers about growing

Growing together

I just can't manage some things yet —
I can't reach the door handle.
I can't see in the bathroom mirror.
I can't always crayon inside the lines.
I can't remember which way round "b" goes.

But one day I will!
One day I'll be bigger than my dad
and then I can do anything!

Please help me, Jesus, while I grow,
to learn fast and work well.
Amen.

Prayers about growing

Being five

Lord Jesus,
I've looked forward to being five
for ever so long.
My brother was five
and I thought I'd catch up
so we'd both be five.
But now I'm five, he's six.
It's not fair...
he's always older than me!
Please help me to enjoy being five anyway.
Amen.

Prayers about growing

Being six

I'm six.
I'm big,
I can skip,
I can click my fingers,
I can count to 100,
I can beat my brother at space invaders!
I can do lots of things!

Thank you, Lord Jesus,
for all the fun of growing up
and learning.
Amen.

MORNING AND EVENING PRAYERS

New day

Sun's up,
new day,
thank you, Lord,
I'm on my way!
Amen.

Help me today

"Courage!" Jesus said. "It is I. Don't be afraid!"
Matthew chapter 14, verse 27

Make today a good day, Father.
Live with me today.
Make me kind, not mean.
Make me helpful, not awkward.
Make me a friend, not an enemy.
Help me, because I want you to be pleased with me today.
Amen.

Dreams

When I wake up in the morning
I know that I was dreaming,
but already I've forgotten.

Half-remembered dreams,
round-the-corner dreams,
just-gone dreams,
nearly dreams.

Lord Jesus, you know my thoughts
even when I'm asleep.
Please take my dreams;
make them happy dreams,
not nightmares.
Take away the things that frighten me.
Give me dreams that make me wake up laughing!
Amen.

Morning and evening prayers

My cuddly

I can't find my cuddly.
He's a rabbit with long ears
and no fur left at all.
Mum says he must be somewhere.
Dad says he's probably hiding.
But it's bedtime, and I want him NOW!
Lord Jesus, please keep my rabbit safe
and bring him back to me soon.
Amen.

Morning and evening prayers

Thank you

Thank you, Father, for my happy day.
Thank you for school,
thank you for play,
thank you for home and television,
thank you that I am warm and safe.
I'm sorry that sometimes I did things wrong.
Please forgive me and help me do better tomorrow.
Amen.

Thank you

Morning and evening prayers

An awful day

It's been an awful day today.
Mum says I got out of bed on the wrong side this morning.
Nothing felt right,
everything itched,
nobody felt right,
I was scratchy and cross.
I didn't want to *be*.

Please help me feel comfortable with myself.
Make tomorrow a happier day.
Amen.

Morning and evening prayers

God is here

When it's dark
and I wiggle my hands in front of my face,
I can feel them here
because they're part of me,
even though I can't see them.

Even though I can't see you, Father God,
I know you're here.
I can feel your kindness sheltering me;
I know that you are real;
I know that you haven't forgotten me.

Thank you, Heavenly Father,
that you are good,
and that you are always with me.
Amen.

PRAYERS ABOUT SPECIAL TIMES

My birthday

Wake up early...
Thank you, Lord,
it's my birthday at last!
I'll go and see if Mum and Dad are awake too...
yes!!
Everyone sings Happy Birthday
to me!
There's a present wrapped in crinkly paper
for me!
Loads of cards come in the post
for me!

Today it's my birthday.
Today I'm the special person.
Everyone smiles and says, "Happy Birthday".
I do love having a birthday.
Thank you, Lord Jesus, for my wonderful day.
Amen.

Prayers about special times

Moving house

We are going to move away from our house.
I hope the new house will be nice
but I don't know yet.

Will you know where I am, Jesus?
Will you hear me from a different town?
But you're always with me,
so you can come too,
then you'll know where I am!
Amen.

Prayers about special times

Christmas

At Christmas we do a play
about the baby Jesus in the stable.
It's cute, with sheep and cows,
stars and kings.

But I like the grown-up Jesus,
who walked around Galilee with fishermen.
He's strong and wise,
kind and funny,
sometimes angry,
always brave.

I like the stories of Jesus in the Bible.
I want to know him better.
Please help me grow up
to be someone like you, Jesus,
kind and brave and wise.
Amen.

Prayers about special times

A sad day

"And God will wipe away every tear from their eyes."
Revelation chapter 7 verse 17

When someone dies,
the person inside has gone away.
My friend died —
I want to talk to him
but he's not there any more.

Why did he die, Jesus?
I'm sure he was happy here with us,
but it must be even nicer with you.

Mum says that nobody cries in heaven.
She says in heaven it's even better than the very best
that I can possibly imagine.

I know you will take care of him, Jesus,
and I'll see him again one day.
Amen.

Prayers about special times

Easter

You're perfect,
so you don't make mistakes,
do you, God?
When Jesus died on the cross
it wasn't a mistake —
it hadn't all gone wrong.

Jesus let himself be taken prisoner.
It was bad when the men
hit him and hurt him
and hung him on the cross,
but it wasn't a mistake —
he did it for me.

Thank you, Jesus.
Amen.